Ink and Beginnings

Ramisa Fariha

BookLeaf Publishing

India | USA | UK

Presentation by *BookLeaf Publishing*

Web: www.bookleafpub.com

E-mail: info@bookleafpub.com

ISBN: 9789363317710

First edition 2024

To

Mahe Jabeen - incredible mother and my moral inspiration

Mir Mashfiqur Rahman - loving brother and my safe space

Mohammed Moin Uddin - thank you for staying by my mom's side

Mohammad Abdul Kader - thank you for my love of learning

Ramisa Fariha (myself) - thank you for staying committed

ACKNOWLEDGEMENT

Opportunity: BookLeaf Publishing

PREFACE

Dear Reader,

These pages are tangible renditions of my voice taking flight. Tentatively, I have expressed my creativity and vulnerability within these verses. As you wander through the pages, listen closely to your own soul---similar echoes of courage and vulnerability may resonate, providing a deeper look into your own symphony.

With these verses, I wish for you to tiptoe along the edges of your memory, where nostalgia blooms and secrets whisper. With each stanza, I invite you to add your voice to the chorus. And if in these pages you find reflections of your own path---the fragile desires, the poignant reveries, and the stubborn magic that resides within us all---I invite you to share such connection with your circle and with me.

Petals

i'm lost here
i'm lost there
i believe i have been lost always
my spirit has forever been part of a time
the doors of which never were opened for me
a deficiency i used to think it
a sadness i must embody day in and day out
lost is a counterpart of adrift you know
as a driftwood recognizes the affection of water
as its roughness explores the forgiving sea
my spirit too has grasped the shroud of my loved
ones
in the passage of time and mistakes
a deficiency i think it not
i've found a home in my spirit
and can you gather she was not lost at all
she had been adrift in this here life's vague
philosophies
moved by a spirit of crushing simplicity
a spirit who wears flowers in her hair

Ink and Ancestry

a   b   c   d
l   n   o   p
somewhere along the way
the l morphed into love for the written word
the n transformed into nanabhai (granpapa)
the o materialized as my observance as you
wrote
the p radiated as my little heart trying her charm
at poetry
your heart and home were filled with books
other worlds i was eager to know
as i begged you for the gift of literacy
you caved by the weight of the worlds around
you
the worlds of poetry, religion, history, law,
pioneers, freedom fighters
the worlds of indignation and understanding
not surprisingly these emotions are my close
companions
as i sat beside you for hours, as you wrote away
for hours
your hands shaking, your stomach rumbling
the thick ink saturating the air, the pen on your
coarse manuscript paper
burning holes in my ears
obsession

Harvest

grim reaper, you left my world with your arms
full
you replaced them with a piece of you
the earth of their graves buried me eight feet
under
their frigidity shattered my reverence
unreachable was i even to Zeus' Thunder
the seasons cycled, i melted

Silent Oaths

i have not never loved
i have not never perched beside a love
questions of a solitary soul
i have not never wrapped my arms around, a
love without a goal
i have not never understood the messages of
love until
forced was i to grasp at the straws
forced was i to shake my soul,
bewildered and forsaken,
"Where were you!" "Where are you!"
calmly, my soul says,
"I have been here, only you were always not."
i have not never felt more horrified and alone
i have not never failed, you know
i have not never failed in my duties to a mother
a principled heart
i have not never failed in my duties to a brother
a trusting core
i have not never failed in my duties to a
grandfather
a solemn soul
i have not never failed in my duties to an aunt
a pristine aura
i have not never failed in my duties to one who

has been my companion through it all
i have not never failed, you know
i have not never felt bitter and alone, you know
i have not never gathered and willed, you know

Maternal Sage

in the midst of studying, Mother asked
if i wanted to visit the mosque and pray
politely i declined, viewing my studying as a
mountain to be climbed
my Mother, gentle and wise,
accepted, leaving me with simple words
allow me to encapsulate
what we prioritize is sacred, but
we must also prioritize what has been sacred
god loved me through his tears
he rained on our home
morphed it into his abode
side by side i prayed with Mother
my sacred soul

Echoes

perhaps you are not deep at all
have you thought about it?
perhaps you are as hollow as you feel
perhaps you are as shallow as you many times
wonder
perhaps you have yourself all wrong, my dear
Or
Or,
perhaps you are as musical as the chords of a
heart
perhaps there is much inside you as a charming,
long book
perhaps you have not got it all wrong

Ink Veiled

writing is my hobby
my mother pointed, "is it truly?"
defensive, I told her of my capers
Mother asks, "can you show me on paper?"
well no, you see
they are my private writings
meant for my opprobrium only
i write crinkled in my snail shell
lightly moving along to slowed down time
incurious of the passerby
uncaring about their position in connection with
me
i have been practicing my love in secrecy

Ascent of Resolve

the future of corrections seems like a mountain
perhaps it is just a molehill
it overwhelms me for a moment, powerless
reorienting my heart will require but a snap of
the fingers
but the system you have placed in me
will not bow down so easily
cogitation of a melancholic moment
i wonder, naturally
i cannot be anything before my time
it is always time to be the best i can
neither i nor another will be a roadblock
to my map of success

Ammu's Lullaby

markings of a fable
nurturing shadow
inspiring breath
multi-faceted, intricately simple
aurora-borealis
markings of a fable
i call my fairy tale Ammu (mother)
my fairy tale calls me Moyna (starling)
markings of a fairytale
humbly hidden in Mother

Yearning's Canopy

i yearn
i yearn
for the flower gardens i will never traverse
for the clans who do not speak my language
for the wild creatures who bound for pleasure
for the bambis and fays of the forests not
destined to cross my path
i yearn for everything i have not known
i yearn for them all from the succor of my
present
my yearning pulls me into nature's embrace
as I meet the sun and the wind
as I meet the freedom loving dragonflies and the
hungry bees
as I crush the feathery orb of a dandelion under
my bare feet
I feel
I feel
I feel the weight of the foreign clans
I feel the liberty of the wild beings
I feel the magic of the forests
I lift my head to the indiscriminate sun and the
adulteress wind
I am whole with everything that has ever been

Self: a Love Letter

when you cannot find me in your heart
take a stroll through the countryside
there i will be
in every birdsong
in every ghostly kiss
in every butterfly
when you miss me dearly
recite the rebel poet
remember his audaciously gentle stand on
liberation
there you will find me
in every nudge to freedom
when you want to learn to love me a little harder
lose your footing in the white sand of padre
surrender to the dichotomy of the crisp provision
and the searing healing
there you will find me
melting
on the boundary of truth and dare

Beneath My Notice

consciously loving
trusting is the essence
solace
friendly conversations
such surface words
so plain
i seek a depth
perhaps no longer seek
"I am fine," I say
"I am fine," he says
further words aren't spoken
are they needed?
it's all a habit
we're all habits

Turbulence

dreams of yesterday
have not fared so well today
will they tomorrow?
is the answer just as denied of truth
as the question?
truth is arrestingly plain
it is beckoning...
purpose beckons the artist
visualize capacity
you have reassembled my notes
but have not poisoned me much
i see the turbulence in you
come rest your mind
brainy yet burning
you are not the only kind
come dish your duty or your sorrow
who knows if you will fare well tomorrow?

Blossoms Unbidden

in the sun-dappled corners of your backyard
growing between your lawn trims
what do you find?
the white and pink flowers you did not plant
the wild mushrooms always a surprise
what do you find?
are they invaders in your eyes as the books say?
or are they the season's enchantments nestled at
the eyes of your heart?

Echoes from the Padma

Padma
swaying atop your grey waters
i've dreamt of sights far from your cool reverie
swaying atop your grey waters
i have been a lone wolf on mount kilimanjaro
i have been a blended tourist at the foot of lady
liberty
i have been a patriot in the alamo
with my eyes lost in dreams far away
your country loving water lilies have passed by
in neglect
your patriotic hilsha have come up for a missed
hello
my boat companion has seemingly been
speaking in tongues
all while my mind has cozied up to the culture of
another
swaying atop the Padma River, yearning for
anything but the present
i have spilled out my roots
becoming emptier than at dreams' beginning

Chronicles of Encounter

it is said that god has created us so that we may
know one another
why does it feel like i have only the met the
worst of us
yet when i think of mother i know i have also
met the best of us

Agony

my brother is sweet
my brother is quietly loving
papa you have missed out on the pride of raising
a compassionate son

Becoming

when the cacophony slumbers
when hope is on full play
i rewrite my history
who shall i be?

Good Bones by Maggie Smith

Life is short, though I keep this from my
children.
Life is short, and I've shortened mine
in a thousand delicious ill-advised ways
a thousand delicious ill-advised ways
I'll keep from my children.
The world is at least fifty percent terrible and
that's a conservative estimate
though I keep this from my children.
For every bird, there is a stone thrown at a bird
For every loved child, a child broken.
Life is short and the world is at least half terrible
and for every kind stranger, there is one who
would break you
though I keep this from my children; I am trying
to sell them the world.
Any decent realtor, walking you through a real
dump,
chirps on about good bones:
this place could be beautiful, right?
you could make this place beautiful.